The Nature Kid's Guide to
CLOWNFISH

DAVID ANDERSON

LP Media Inc. Publishing
Text copyright © 2026 by LP Media Inc.

For information address LP Media Inc. Publishing,
30012 Variolite St NW, Princeton MN 55371
www.lpmedia.org

Publication Data

Clownfish
The Nature Kid's Guide to Clownfish — First edition.

Summary: "Learn all about Clownfish, the Nature Kid Way"
— Provided by publisher.

ISBN: 979-8-89818-234-2

[1. Clownfish – Non-Fiction] I. Title.

Title: The Nature Kid's Guide to Clownfish

CONTENTS

CORAL CRIBS

DID YOU KNOW?
A clownfish almost never swims more than a few feet from its anemone home!

Splash! A bright orange fish darts into a sea anemone.

Clownfish live in warm ocean water. They make their homes on **coral reefs**—underwater cities built by tiny animals called coral.

These little fish live inside **sea anemones**. An anemone looks like a flower, but it is actually an animal! It has soft arms that wave in the water.

A clownfish and its anemone are partners. They help each other stay safe and healthy. This team is one of nature's best pairs, and they can stay together for years.

WORLD WIDE

No clownfish have ever been found in the Atlantic Ocean—not even one!

Swoosh! A clownfish zips through a warm tropical reef.

Clownfish live in the Indian and Pacific Oceans. You can find them near Australia, Japan, and India. They love warm, sunny water near the equator.

These fish do not live in cold seas. You will not spot one near the North Pole! They need warm reefs to survive, with water between 75 and 82 degrees.

Some clownfish stay in shallow water close to shore. Others swim deeper, down to 40 feet. But no matter where they live, they always stick close to a reef.

TINY TOTS

The most common clownfish weighs less than half an ounce—lighter than a AA battery.

Pop! A tiny clownfish peeks out from waving tentacles.

There are around 30 different kinds of clownfish, and they come in many colors and patterns. Most grow to be about three or four inches long — roughly the size of your finger!

The smallest clownfish are barely two inches long. You could hold one in the palm of your hand. But the biggest ones, like maroon clownfish, can grow over six inches!

Female clownfish grow bigger than males. In each group, the mom is always the largest fish. She can be twice the size of the dad!

FIN FACTS

DID YOU KNOW?
Not all clownfish are orange.
Some are red, yellow,
brown, or even black!

Flip! A clownfish fans its fins and glides through the water.

Clownfish have round, flat bodies. Bright orange scales make them easy to spot. White stripes with black edges mark their skin like bold racing stripes.

These fish have several fins to help them move. A tall fin on their back helps them steer. Two side fins push them forward, and a tail fin gives them speed.

Clownfish have big round eyes and a small mouth. Their eyes help them watch for danger from many directions at once. Those sharp eyes can spot a predator before it gets close!

SUPER
SENSES

FUN
FACT!

Clownfish make popping
and clicking sounds to talk
to each other!

Click! A clownfish hears a snapping shrimp on the reef.

Clownfish can hear sounds in the water. They pick up clicks and pops from the busy reef. They even make their own sounds by snapping their jaws!

These fish can smell very well, too. They use smell to find their way home. A clownfish can sniff out its own anemone from far away, even in murky water!

Clownfish also see in color. Their big eyes spot movement fast. Good eyes, ears, and a sharp nose all work together to help them stay safe in the sea.

SLIME SHIELD
The slime on a clownfish is three to four times thicker than on other fish.
DID YOU KNOW?
14

Poof! A clownfish dives right into stinging anemone arms.

Sea anemones sting most fish that touch them. But not clownfish! They have a secret weapon—a thick coat of slime that covers their whole body.

This slime is like a magic shield. It stops the anemone's sting from hurting them. Without this slime, a clownfish would get zapped just like any other fish!

Baby clownfish build up their slime slowly. They rub against the anemone a little at a time. Soon their slime coat is thick enough to keep them safe for life.

LUNCH MENU

DID YOU KNOW?
Clownfish poop helps feed their anemone. It is like paying rent with fertilizer!

Gulp! A clownfish swallows a tiny piece of floating algae.

Clownfish eat many kinds of food. They munch on **algae**, which are tiny plants in the sea. They also eat bits of shrimp and other small creatures.

These fish snack on leftovers from their anemone, too. When the anemone catches food, bits fall off. The clownfish gobbles up the scraps like a helpful roommate!

Clownfish also eat **plankton**—tiny living things that float in the water. They nibble a little bit all day long instead of eating big meals.

GRAB GRUB

FUN
FACT!
Clownfish sometimes fan water toward their anemone to bring it food—like room service!

Snap! A clownfish darts out and snatches a bit of food.

Clownfish do not hunt like big fish do. They do not chase their food very far. Instead, they grab whatever drifts close by.

When a tasty bit floats near, the clownfish zips out. It grabs the food with a quick snap. Then it swims right back to safety in its anemone.

Clownfish also pick at algae growing on nearby rocks. They take small bites all through the day. With food always floating by, they never have to go far for a meal.

DANGER ZONE

DID YOU KNOW?
A moray eel can be six feet long—that is 20 times longer than a clownfish!

Zoom! A clownfish spots a moray eel heading toward its home.

The ocean is a scary place for small clownfish. Moray eels are one of their scariest enemies. These sneaky eels slide into tight reef spaces looking for a meal.

Big groupers also hunt clownfish. Barracudas can zip by and snatch one up in a flash. Even some sharks will eat a clownfish if they get close enough.

Danger can come from all sides. Clownfish must always be on the lookout. Being a small fish in the big ocean is not easy!

HIDE FAST

FUN FACT!
A clownfish will even nip at a scuba diver who gets too close to its home!

Zip! A clownfish shoots back into its anemone to hide.

When danger comes, clownfish dive deep into their anemone. They tuck themselves into the stinging **tentacles** where no predator can follow. It is the perfect hiding spot!

But clownfish are also brave fighters. If something gets too close, they rush out and charge at it! They puff up their bodies and nip with their tiny teeth.

When the whole family works together, most enemies swim away. Even the smallest clownfish will join a fight. These tiny fish have big courage!

WIGGLE SWIM

Clownfish are one of the slowest swimming fish on a coral reef—but they do not need speed!

Splish! A clownfish wiggles its body and strolls across the reef.

Clownfish swim in a funny way. They wiggle their bodies side to side. This is not the fastest way to swim, but it works for them!

Most fish glide smoothly through the water. Not clownfish. Their bodies rock back and forth like a little boat on waves. Scientists call this a "waddle."

Luckily, clownfish do not need to travel far. They stay within a few feet of their anemone. Home is always just a short swim away.

DAY LIFE

In the wild, some clownfish can live for 10 years or more—longer than most pet dogs!

Blub! A clownfish wakes up and begins its busy day on the reef.

A clownfish has a busy day. Each morning, it swims around its home and checks on things. It makes sure all is safe and sound.

During the day, clownfish clean their anemone. They nibble off dead bits and push away old food. This keeps their home neat and healthy for both partners.

At night, clownfish settle down to rest. They tuck into the soft tentacles of their anemone. The reef gets quiet, and the little fish drifts off to sleep.

FAMILY FISH
FUN FACT!
A clownfish group usually has between two and six fish—but only one female.

Thwack! The lead clownfish bumps a smaller fish back into line.

Clownfish live in small groups. Each group shares one anemone home. The group has a strict order, and every fish knows its place.

The female runs the show. She is the biggest and the boss. The male is her partner and second in charge. The rest of the fish follow their lead.

If a smaller fish breaks the rules, the leaders chase it. This might seem mean, but it keeps the group safe and organized. Order is very important in a clownfish family!

LOVE DANCE

A male clownfish can change into a female if the female dies—but it cannot change back!

Swish! Two clownfish circle each other in a graceful dance.

When it is time to mate, clownfish put on a show. The male swims around the female. He bobs up and down and shows off his fins.

The pair swims close together. They lean toward each other and chase each other around. It looks like they are doing a funny little dance!

This dance is how clownfish show they are ready to be parents. The male works hard to get the female's attention. If she likes his dance, they become a pair for life!

TINY FRY
DID YOU KNOW?
A female clownfish can lay up to 1,000 eggs at a single time!
32

Stay back! A clownfish protects his newly laid eggs.

The female clownfish lays many tiny eggs. She puts them on a flat rock near the anemone. The eggs are very small—about the size of rice grains.

The eggs take about one week to hatch. At first they are bright orange. As the babies grow inside, the eggs turn dark and you can see tiny eyes!

When the eggs hatch, tiny baby fish called fry swim out. They are so small you can almost see through them. The fry float away into the open water to start their own adventures.

DAD DUTY

Clownfish eggs hatch at night when it is dark—this helps the tiny fry hide from predators.

Flap! The dad clownfish fans the eggs with his strong fins.

In most fish families, no one watches the eggs. But clownfish dads are different. The dad guards the nest day and night for a whole week!

He fans the eggs with his fins to bring fresh water to them. He also picks off any eggs that go bad. This hard work keeps the healthy eggs safe and growing.

The dad does not eat much while he guards the eggs. He stays close until every baby has hatched. Clownfish dads are some of the best fathers in the sea!

REEF RISK

DID YOU KNOW?

After the movie Finding Nemo came out, pet stores sold 40% more clownfish!

Gurgle! A clownfish watches as warm water turns the coral white.

Clownfish need healthy coral reefs to live. But many reefs are in trouble. When the water gets too warm, coral turns white and dies. This is called coral bleaching.

Pollution hurts reefs, too. Trash and dirty water can kill the coral and anemones. When coral dies, the fish that depend on it are in danger.

Some people also catch wild clownfish to sell as pets. Taking too many from the wild is a big problem. Wild clownfish need to stay where they belong—on the reef.

SAVE SEAS
FUN FACT!
Some groups raise clownfish in tanks so wild ones do not need to be caught—you can buy tank-raised pets!
38

Plop! A clownfish swims past a spot where new coral is growing.

People around the world are working to save coral reefs. Scientists grow new coral in labs and plant it in the sea. This helps damaged reefs grow back.

Many countries have made rules to protect reefs, too. Some places do not allow fishing near coral. Marine parks keep large areas safe for sea life.

You can help! Use less plastic. Pick up trash near the beach. Tell your friends about clownfish. Every small act can make a big difference for the ocean and the amazing animals that call it home.

GLOSSARY

coral reef

An underwater structure built by tiny sea animals.

sea anemone

A soft sea animal with stinging tentacles that looks like a flower.

tentacles

Long, soft arms on a sea animal used for stinging or grabbing.

algae

Tiny plant-like living things that grow in water.

plankton

Very tiny living things that float in the ocean.